A catalogue record for this book is available from the British Library

Based on the motion picture screenplay by David Koepp
Based on the novel THE LOST WORLD by Michael Crichton

Published by Ladybird Books Ltd
A subsidiary of the Penguin Group
A Pearson Company

LADYBIRD and the device of a Ladybird are trademarks of
Ladybird Books Ltd Loughborough Leicestershire UK

Ladybird

Nikon

Dr Ian Malcolm took a deep breath and stepped off the boat at the edge of a tropical lagoon. He watched as the trailer backed down a narrow ramp. Nick Van Owen, the cameraman, and Eddie Carr, the equipment specialist, were the only other people involved in this expedition. They were here to observe and record dinosaur life on the island. Ian was here to find Sarah.

Sarah Harding was a scientist sent to Isla Sorna by John Hammond, the creator of Jurassic Park, to study the behaviour of dinosaurs on this lost world. Sarah was also Ian's girlfriend. When Hammond told him Sarah was on Isla Sorna, Ian decided to go there and bring her back home. Ian knew she was in a lot of danger.

And now, to make matters worse, his daughter Kelly had stowed away, hoping for adventure and determined to spend time with her father. "Some adventure," Ian muttered, shaking his head in despair.

As the boat pulled away, the small party made their way into the jungle. They hadn't travelled far when they spotted Sarah. She had been watching a herd of Stegosaurs and now a baby in the group was busy watching Sarah! As they joined her, they heard the sound of helicopters. InGen had arrived...

InGen was a company with only one purpose – making huge amounts of money. The company had come to the island to capture the dinosaurs in order to create a dinosaur zoo. Ian, Kelly, Sarah, Nick and Eddie set out in the direction the helicopters had gone.

They came to a ridge overlooking a wide open field. They looked down and couldn't believe their eyes. There seemed to be some kind of high-tech dinosaur rodeo going on! Specially made trucks were racing through the field, chasing dinosaurs and trying to lasso them. Terrified dinosaurs were running in every direction. Ian, Kelly, Sarah, Nick and Eddie watched in horror as one of the hunters managed to capture a young Pachycephalosaurus. Another hunter took aim and shot it with a tranquillizer gun. Within minutes, the limp, stunned Pachycephalosaurus had been loaded into a cage and the chase continued.

Throughout the day, more and more dinosaurs were captured. One of the hunters even managed to catch a baby Tyrannosaurus Rex. The tiny creature was taken back to the InGen base camp and chained to a stake. As it stood there, frightened and screaming, the hunters hoped that it would attract the most valuable prey of all – an adult T-Rex.

Later that night, Sarah and Nick sneaked into the InGen camp to free the trapped dinosaurs. As the hunters slept, Nick cut through the chains and Sarah opened all the cage doors. All of a sudden, the animals were loose. In their panic, the dinosaurs ran through the camp, trampling tents and smashing equipment. The hunters, awakened by all the noise, leapt from their camp beds and scrambled for cover. They hadn't bargained on this in the middle of the night!

Smiling at the success of their mission, Sarah and Nick headed back to their own camp. Suddenly, they spotted the baby T-Rex. As Sarah bent to free the creature, she noticed that its leg had been broken. "We have to do something, Nick," she whispered. "If this bone isn't set, it will never heal properly. He won't survive!"

Nick picked up the screaming baby T-Rex and they ran for their trailer. "He's too loud! He's going to wake the whole jungle," Nick warned as they raced into the trailer with the howling animal.

"He's in pain. It won't take long to get the leg set. Then we'll let him go," said Sarah, and she began to splint the baby dinosaur's broken bone.

The baby dinosaur continued to loudly howl his protests as Sarah fixed his leg. However, just as she put the last of the sticking plaster on the splint, the trailer began to shake. Sarah and Nick looked at each other – they had no idea what was happening. Suddenly, Ian burst into the trailer. "Get that thing out of here! Now!" he yelled.

"What is it?" Sarah asked.

"It's Mummy and Daddy!" Ian told her as he grabbed the small, struggling dinosaur and ran towards the door. Two adult T-Rexes were just outside. They could see their baby through the trailer windows, and Sarah could see two very large mouths with huge teeth! The T-Rexes roared with rage, frantic to get their stolen baby back.

Ian quickly opened the door. The small dinosaur struggled out of his arms onto the ground, and began to gurgle. When the adult T-Rexes saw their baby, they stopped roaring and began to gurgle as well. Glad to be together again, the three dinosaurs moved off into the jungle. Ian, Sarah and Nick sighed with relief. That had been a close call!

Sarah was beginning to wonder if this trip to study dinosaur behaviour had been such a good idea after all.

"It's time to get out of here," Ian said, waiting for an argument.

Nick looked at him. "I agree."

"Me, too," Sarah nodded. "Let's find Kelly and Eddie and go home."

Nick turned on the radio to signal the boat to pick them up. Then the trailer began to shake. The T-Rexes weren't finished with them yet. Before Ian could send the signal, there was a huge crash. The trailer turned over on its side and began to move. "They're pushing us!" Ian yelled. "And we're headed straight for the cliff!"

Just then, Eddie appeared outside the broken window of the trailer. "They haven't seen me," he whispered. "Take the end of this rope. I've tied it to a tree."

All three grabbed the rope just as the trailer slid off the cliff to the rocks below. The T-Rexes turned towards the jungle and saw Eddie. One of them seized him in its mouth and threw him in the air. As he screamed, both giant heads lunged at him and he disappeared between their teeth! Then the two dinosaurs moved off into the jungle.

Sarah, Nick and Ian clung to the rope, dangling above the smashed trailer. They slowly began to pull themselves up when suddenly, a hand appeared over the edge of the cliff. It was one of the hunters. He pulled them to safety where Kelly was waiting, her eyes wide with fear. This wasn't the kind of adventure she'd imagined! Without speaking, they followed the hunter back to what was left of the InGen camp.

Neither of the groups had any equipment left. It had all been destroyed by the dinosaurs. They had no radio to signal for help. But they had a map. Near the middle of the island was a village. It was deserted now, mostly destroyed by a hurricane, but it held a communication station – and a radio. The weary survivors set out on the long journey to the village.

After several hours of walking through the thick jungle, the ground began to tremble again. The T-Rexes had decided that they didn't want these humans on their island any more!

Everyone in the party scattered, running through the jungle to escape the angry dinosaurs. They reached a ravine with the T-Rexes close behind. As they ran in terror, Nick saw a waterfall with an opening behind it. He grabbed Kelly and Sarah and they ran to the waterfall.

"Jump!" Nick yelled, and they all leapt into the falling water – and through it – into a tiny cave. They pressed themselves flat against the back of the cave as the dinosaur chase continued, holding their breath as they heard the terrified screams of the unlucky hunters who were unable to escape the anger of the mighty T-Rexes.

After what seemed like a very long time, the jungle outside grew quiet again. Sarah, Nick and Kelly stepped back out into the ravine and saw Ian. He ran to Kelly and hugged her, glad that she was still alive. Ian turned to Nick and thanked him – he had saved Kelly and Sarah's lives. The hunters who had survived the attack had long since gone on their way towards the village. Now the four of them were all alone.

Ian, Kelly, Sarah and Nick carried on, making their way through the jungle. Meanwhile, the hunters had finally stopped running and, laughing with relief, had stopped at the edge of a field of tall grass. They looked around them, all was still. The fearsome T-Rexes were far behind. The hunters had survived!

The small band of men began to cross the field in single file, blindly pushing their way through the grass which was taller than themselves.

Silently, a small head with large menacing eyes rose above the grass. Then another. And another. Unfortunately for the hunters, they had stumbled across the nesting ground of a herd of Velociraptors! And it was now feeding time for these small but fast meat-eaters. On all sides, the grass rippled as the raptors moved swiftly and silently towards their prey.

The last hunter in line suddenly disappeared without a noise. The group moved on, not knowing the danger they were in. The next hunter disappeared as suddenly as the first, then the next. One by one the raptors picked off the hunters.

Completely unaware of the feeding frenzy, the hunter at the head of the line turned to the man behind him, only to see a raptor springing out of the grass at him. He screamed for a second. Then all was silent.

By the time Ian, Kelly, Nick and Sarah reached the clearing at the end of the tall grass, it was, once more, a quiet, peaceful field. Just like the hunters, they started to cross it. They hadn't gone far when Ian heard a familiar snarl. He stopped and looked around him. Then he saw the tall grass shivering. Ian knew instantly the danger they were in – raptors were no strangers to him.

"Run! Run as fast as you can! Go!" he shouted, and they all raced blindly through the field. Suddenly the ground disappeared beneath their feet and they were tumbling down a steep, rocky hillside.

When they got to the bottom, Nick got to his feet shakily and dusted off his trousers as he looked around. They were just outside the village. "Is everyone all right?" he asked, offering Sarah a hand.

"No," said Ian. "I think I've broken my leg." His leg was twisted at an odd angle beneath him.

"Nick, you go ahead," Sarah told him. "You're the fastest runner of all of us. Get to the communication centre and radio for help. Kelly and I will stay with Ian."

Nick raced off into the darkness as Ian slowly got to his feet. He leaned on Sarah for support and the three of them headed off after Nick. They hadn't gone far when there was a blinding light. The communication station was lit up like a beacon just ahead. Ian, Kelly and Sarah sighed with relief.

They struggled towards the building ahead of them. Then they heard it – the snarl they all recognized. There was a raptor behind them!

InGen
We Make Your Future

"Come on!" Sarah cried, pulling the limping Ian with her.

"No – you two go. You'll never make it with me," Ian said, pushing Sarah away.

"No way!" Sarah yelled, pulling Ian along behind her. "Run!" They ran towards the building as quickly as they could, the snarling raptor close behind. They reached the door. Frantically, Sarah pulled Kelly and Ian inside, then threw her back against the door with a thud. The raptor slammed into the outside of the door, screaming with fury.

Meanwhile, Nick had managed to get through to InGen on the radio and help was on its way. Soon an InGen helicopter descended on the roof of the building.

Within seconds, the survivors were loaded aboard and the helicopter took off, leaving the lost world behind, for ever!

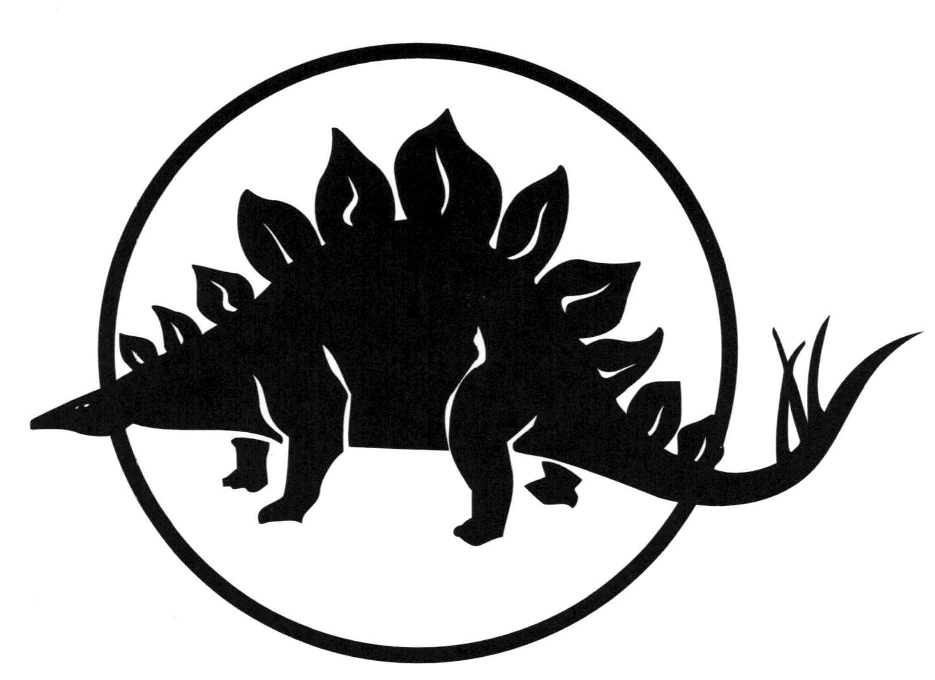